Angel Reiki Course Manual

Bertena Varney

Published by Bertena Varney, 2022.

Angel Reiki Course Manual

Disclaimer

This book does not hold any claim to heal anyone or anything. This is simply a meditation session that allows the body to relax and to heal themselves. This is NOT to take the place of medical or psychiatric help. These should come first, and the author holds no responsibility for anything that the reader of this book may do.

Introduction

Welcome to Angel Reiki Master Certification Class. This manual is part of the class that I teach in person, online, and as a correspondence course. If you are interested in receiving the attunement, then there are 2 options that are offered – just the attunement sent distantly or enrollment in the online class. Please see the last chapter for specifics.

I am glad you have chosen to learn this Reiki energy modality that I channeled and have taught to numerous students. Each of these specific energy modalities appear to fit perfectly together; and, with the guidance of the Archangels, has really worked with my experiences to create an energy modality that is just prefect for working with them.

Students working with this manual will see that the lessons focus first on learning how to connect with your archangels, then you will learn how to work with the energy, how to connect with your client and finally how to physically work with your clients. As the class progresses students will be introduced to the more intuitive based lessons such as reading angel cards, past life readings, aura readings and chakra balancing and much more.

Once you complete this class, you will then receive a distant attunement from me. After the attunements, you are ready to work on yourself and others. You can add this energy work to your established profession or begin a new business working with angels. Also, you will be ready to add your intuition to the energy work. This could include readings of past lives, angel card readings and more.

You are encouraged, once you receive the attunements, to continue practicing in the step-by-step way that is taught in this class. Once you are comfortable with your interaction with the Archangels and have confidence in yourself, then you may take these lessons and make it your own technique. In other words, you may create sessions that fit the path that you are on, as well as adapting this energy modality in a way that it will benefit your clients.

So, if you are ready, we can begin the class.

What are Energy Modalities?

Energy modalities, such as Reiki, Qigong, yoga, pranic healing, healing touch, or just good old-fashioned faith healing, have been around since the beginning of time. African tribes used animal energy, or what they called magnetism, to help heal their warriors or people in their tribes. The Japanese introduced Reiki to the eastern world and then later in the western hemisphere as a "universal energy" that heals through the universe. These are all still in practice today.

When you study each of the ancient or modern traditions, you will notice that there is one thing in common among them. You will find that universal energy travels through the student, heals the student where needed and then it travels to the client or person receiving the energy. Many people ask if there is enough energy to do this and the answer is yes.

As said above, some modalities have energy coming from an outside source (archangels, universe, God, etc.) while others bring it from inside of them. No matter where it comes from, energy is abundant and, as physicists have proven, energy can neither be created nor destroyed. It is abundant and forever available, so you will never run out of energy.

In the end it is not which energy modality is the right one to use but which one is right for you. Remember that this is not a substitution for medical or psychiatric help. This is based on faith and allowing your body to relax and help it become better. Let us continue to learn what Angel Reiki is.

What is Angel Reiki?

Angel Reiki is a complementary energy modality where the practitioner learns to work with the Archangels Michael, Raphael, Gabriel, and Uriel. Students learn what each archangel represents and how they help you find and heal yourself or your client. Students will also learn about their "clairs" and how they will communicate with the angels.

When working with the archangels, students wonder where angels come from, are they doing right by working with them and worry about ego-based fears. The following paragraphs address these concerns and more.

First, angels are nondenominational, they are not solely "Christian". Angels are found in Judaism, Islam, Christianity, as well as voodoo, indigenous religions in Africa, and even in some eastern religions. So, they will respond to you whether you are a certain religion or no religion at all. Just remember that they are spiritual beings that are here to help us, but they will never try to change your free will.

Secondly, know that we do not control angels. We are not over them and they do not control us either. They are messengers and protectors, and they are willing to help us if we ask, but we must ask for their help. And as a side note, angels cannot harm anyone.

Third, they are spiritual beings and are not bound by time and space. You can ask Archangel Michael for help, and he can also be across the world or next door helping someone else at that same moment. So, do not feel like you are going to take him away from someone if you ask for his help. He can be in many places at one time. It is hard for us to comprehend but have faith and simply ask for his help.

Fourth, many people ask if we are worshipping angels and the answer is no. We are simply talking to them and asking for their help. They are here to help and guide us. God created them so that they could bring us messages and help guide us on the right path.

And the last question that I am often asked is what do angels look like? Well, remember that archangels are the warriors of the angel realms, and they are big and strong looking. They are not weak and fragile but are still very comforting to us. To many people they may only see colors, or they may see a full shape or the full angel; these changes depend upon each person. Angels appear differently to different people. Please do not assume that they all have wings or are cute and cuddly. Angels are a force to be reckoned with and can take the form of humans if they need to. When communicating with angels we get lots of feelings as to whether they have male or female energy. Technically, angels do not have gender, but Archangel Michael is almost always identified as male and Jophiel and Uriel as females. So, remember to trust what you see, hear, and feel.

Are you ready to get started learning how to heal with the archangels?

Who are the Archangels?

There are 9 levels of angels: Seraphim, Cherubim, Thrones, Dominions, Virtues, Powers, Principalities, Archangels, and Guardian Angels.

The 1st Triad lives in the highest realm of heaven:

> Seraphim are the angels that are closest to God, are pure light and are the highest order of angels. They sing Holy, holy, holy and have 6 sets of wings. 2 around their feet, 2 around their chest and 2 around their faces.

> Cherubim are the second highest order and are pure love. wo pairs of wings, and four faces: that of a lion that representative wild anima), an ox that represents domesticated animals, a human, and an eagle that represents all birds.

> Thrones are the connection between heaven and our world and oversee fairness and justice from God. They are very much like Wisemen of the time

The 2nd Triad are between earth and heaven:

> Dominions manage the angels according to God's will. They look more of how we tend to think of angels.

> Virtues rule over the sun, moon, stars and all the planets.

> Powers are peaceful warriors, and they help clean the lower energies on the earthly plane. They take care of negative energy, as well as negative entities.

The 3rd Triad are closest to Earth:

> Principalities watch over earth and are the ones that help with "peace on Earth". We see these as the angels at Christmas and they help in violent situations. Many times, the have scepters and a crown.

> Archangels oversee humans and guardian angels. They each represent an aspect of God. They are here to help us and are the ones that we are going to learn about in this class. There are said to only be 7- Michael Gabriel, Uriel, Ariel, Chamuel, Jophiel and Zadkiel. They are spoke about in the book of Revelations and the Book of Enoch.

> Guardian Angels are our personal angels assigned to us in our life. Each person is born with two guardian angels and gain and lose them throughout our life depending upon when or if we need them.

There are angels for everything: abundance, wellness, romance, fitness, nature- everything. So, remember that no matter what situation you are in, there are angels everywhere.

Here are the Archangels that we will use in this class:

Michael is the warrior archangel, and his name means "He who is as God". He oversees protecting us and the world and is here to help us when we are scared for our safety and/or major changes are occurring in our lives. Michael helps when the client is wanting to let go of something or someone or wants to change their life. He is great with life path work and gives you the courage to do what you want. He is the patron archangel of police and military, and, surprisingly, works with mechanical and electrical issues (things that help us succeed in life). He is super strong and is the most called upon angel. Michael helps protect us from energies that may come from our client as well as give us strength to help our clients. Colors associated with Michael are gold and white.

Raphael is the second angel that we will work with here. Raphael is the wellness angel, and his name means "God heals" the mind, body, and soul of humans and animals. He is also great with education, traveling, health and finding your way so that you are happy in your life. When you are happy in your life you usually become healthier. Raphael is the angel who helps you know where to heal and how to heal your clients. He will help guide your hand and the energy to where it needs to go. The colors associated with Raphael are green and pink.

Gabriel is the "messenger of God" and has the familiarity of giving off female energy but has been called a male and female. Gabriel is the archangel that delivered the news of baby Jesus and his cousin John the Baptist. Because of this, Gabriel is the archangel that we turn to for help with pregnancy, births, and child related issues. She helps writers, teachers, artists, journalists, and anyone who needs help with creativity. Gabriel helps with overcoming fear and writer's block. Gabriel will be the angel who, in the second level, will help you do card or past life readings as well as help you to know what to say to your client to help them heal. Gabriel's colors are blue and indigo.

Uriel is the final major archangel that you will ask for help from in the second level. Uriel means "God is light" and helps you see the situation and solve the problem. After Gabriel tells you or the client their issue, then Uriel will help you think clearly and find the answers. Uriel is more logically based and helps you look at things in a more logical and grounded way. The colors associated with Uriel are red and orange.

Other archangels that you may connect and work with may include:

Ariel oversees the health of the Earth. She helps with the elemental kingdom and animals. Ariel helps you communicate with the fae/fairy, so if you are working with fae/fairy she can help. She helps us with environmental concerns and helps heal the Earth and in turn helps heal us.

Azrael is the Archangel of Death, but I like to think of him as the angel of changes or transitions and passing of old memories, habits, and transitioning to other planes. He also helps with spiritual counseling and comforting your client. Many people fear Azrael but that is not necessary, he is simply doing a job that many angels do not want to do.

Chamuel helps us find out new interests, friendships, loves and even lost items. He helps with misunderstandings and confusions in relationships. He is very loving and kind and will lead you to your soul mate.

Haniel is the archangel of peace, serenity, beauty, harmony, and grace. Haniel helps you when you must give presentations, or interview or teach. He helps you to not be as nervous and gives you peace before you do it.

Jeremiel helps us with emotional wellness and forgiveness of others. He helps us learn about ourselves by serving others. Jeremiel helps us see the darkness that we have walked through and, in turn, helps the light begin to heal and radiate from us.

Jophiel is the watcher of artists and of beauty. She helps make the world beautiful by touching our projects, cleaning our environment, or getting it straight, kind of like Feng Shui. She helps put us in order so that we may grow spiritually. She will help if you have writer's block or lose that inspiration on the project you were working on.

Metatron is one of the more controversial archangels. He is the youngest and tallest of the angels and it is said that he was Enoch – a human from earth. This is controversial to most people because angels are a different species, we are not to interbreed with angels, and we do not become one when we die. This was a very special circumstance. Metatron is one of two that has been blessed to become an angel. More importantly, he is the head angel on the Tree of Life and helps Mary with the Indigo and Crystal Children. He is the angel of education as well.

Raguel is the archangel of justice and helps you gain strength when you feel out of balance and off center. He helps with bullying and uneven relationships. He helps you to overcome the darkness of revenge by giving you strength to let it go and let God deal with it.

Raziel is the archangel that stands near to God. He knows all the secrets and mysteries of God. He wrote down the secrets and gave them to Enoch and to Samuel. He helps you understand dreams, alchemy, past lives, and manifesting. He is great to use with anything dealing with the Law of Attraction, dream interpretation, and past life regressions. He can help to reveal lessons from your client's life through the cards.

Sandalphon is like Metatron in that he was once human and was known as the prophet Elijah. He is the archangel of music and helps you when you are confused spiritually. He is great to use for teenagers and their moodiness as well.

Zadkiel is the archangel of good memory, helps students' study and helps you concentrate on your memory of where your path is and where you are going. He is great for life path readings.

Assignment:

Find an angel journal if you are doing the correspondence course or complete the work in the online classroom if you are taking the class online. Begin by taking a moment to meditate on the various angels mentioned above. Think about which ones you resonate with. Once you have chosen one or two, research more about them and write about them in your Angel Journal. Think about which ones you want to work with in your daily life and then ask them to help you with your journey.

Archangel Symbols

The symbols from left to right are Michael, Raphael, Uriel, and Gabriel

We ask that you attune to Michael and Raphael during this first level and Uriel and Gabriel in the second level

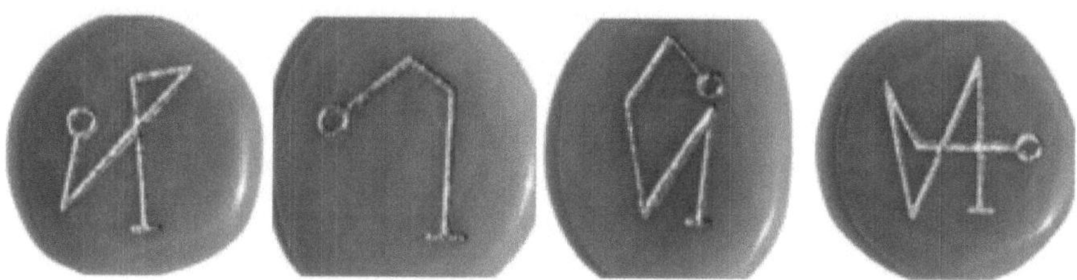

Communicating with the Archangels.

How do you communicate with angels? How do you know if that is an angel that you are interacting with? How do you know if you are seeing them? There are so many questions regarding how to communicate with angels that they all cannot be answered, so I will address the main ones.

First question I get asked is, should we be talking with angels at all? Well, if you remember that they are God's messengers and that they do His will then this will help a lot. You cannot command an angel, but you can ask for guidance and assistance. You also cannot expect them to do things without you asking; they will not violate your self will, so you do have to ask for help when you need it.

Second, ask yourself, "Do you really want to communicate with angels?" Many times, we think we do; but, when the time comes, we get scared, or we do not feel as if we are ready. If we have doubt, they will not force us to hear or to see them, but they will let it happen when you are ready. Do not feel bad if you are not ready, it may take time for you to become comfortable. Simply look for signs, such as feathers or music, and then listen quietly for the message. It may be a feeling in your gut or a quick change in decision that makes you comfortable and feel positive energy. If you do not feel it, then do not push, it will come when you are ready. When you know your intention for wanting to talk to the angels and combine that with the intention of your client's desire for the session, this will allow you to communicate with the angels and to focus your energy where their intention is.

Third, many people ask me how I know that it is an angel that I am speaking to and not something bad? Well, ask yourself if the energy feels bad? If not, then it is a positive being. Next, ask yourself if it is telling you to do something that you feel comfortable with? If so, then it is positive, if it is telling you to harm someone then it is not an angel. Also, if it uses "I" or "we" it is an angel, as compared to messages using the less ego centered words like "us"?

Remember also, if you are talking to angels, they are less emotional and do not have a human personality. If they seem like your grandfather or grandmother, and they have a human personality, it is probably a deceased loved one that you are tapping into. And finally, remember that positive messages are from angels. They can even warn you of things in a positive way but will never send you messages that are fear or threat-based. Ask for a sign from the angels if you are still unsure. It may be a song on the radio, a commercial or even a person that comes into your life or says something that confirms what you think is a message. They are all around us.

Fourth, simply relax and let yourself go. I know that this sounds simple but if you are uptight then it is hard to connect to the angels. Try to relax by playing meditation music or sit on the floor and get comfortable. You do not have to sit upright and perfect, just let go and "be". It will all happen naturally. Many times, ego tries to get in your way and will tell you that "this isn't right", "I'm hearing things", or "why can I do this". These are all doubts that the ego pushes into our mind. We must have faith in ourselves and trust that we are doing what we are supposed to do and that the angels are guiding us.

Fifth, take a moment and look at your life. Are you eating healthy? Is your life in order? Are you are distracted? If you are dealing with issues within yourself then it is hard to help others. We are not saying that you must be "perfectly" healthy, but we are saying that you need to be aware and working with yourself. When you are emotionally happy or physically healthy, then you can concentrate on helping others. As a habit, exercise regularly, eat better and talk to someone to help balance your emotional health. Once you are settled then it will work out and you will be able to connect to the archangels. What you may notice in doing your Reiki or reading sessions is that you may get several clients in one day that have the same issue. This is interesting, but what is more interesting is that, many times, these Reiki sessions, and messages are not only for the clients. You may notice at the beginning that many of these messages relate to you, the healer, at that time as well. Angels speak to us and know what we need to heal so that we can heal others.

The sixth thing that will help you communicate is to practice; practice with your friends, family and even do free readings online. The most important thing that you can do to make yourself comfortable is practice, and the more comfortable you are, the easier it is for you to connect with the angels. You will only become more confident and more confident with our energy modality if you practice. And finally, do not forget to prepare your home.

How Do You Communicate?

There are five ways to receive messages from angels and these are called "clairs." Each person will have one main clair, or way that they receive messages, but over time, and with practice, you will notice that the other clairs will slowly become stronger. Here are the five clairs. Which one is your strongest?

Clairvoyance is the ability to see angels. If you are clairvoyant, then you may only see flashes, shadows, sparkles, light, color, angel clouds, or simply see visions in your mind's eye. Sometimes you may see these items or visions over and over and this is angels trying to communicate with you. Stop and pay attention to repetitive messages. You may also see angels through dreams, daydreaming or even in scrying. Scrying is seeing messages in pictures, numbers, etc.

So, how do you make your clairvoyance stronger? Practice scrying or looking for symbols everywhere, like clouds, tea, mirrors, anywhere that you can see patterns, letters, or numbers. Once you see these patterns, then concentrate on what you see and how it relates to the question now. Does it answer the question or lead to more questions? Many times, when we are doing readings or Reiki for others, we interpret these pictures, symbols or items based on our experience not your clients and this, in turn, can cause issues. For example, if you see the word or a picture of a ball, you may think of a beach ball and the good times that people have at the beach, but when you tell your client that you see a ball they may think of a baseball or basketball, and it may bring a totally different feeling or message to your client. You should always remind your client that you are just the messenger, and it is up to them to take your visions and interpret them so that they relate to their life. Because it is their message from the angels, and you are just the conduit.

Here is an exercise to open your third eye. Make sure that you feel comfortable in seeing and that you have affirmed that you can do this. Next, take a clear quartz crystal and place it to your third eye and then imagine a powerful beam of light coming into your eyes. Next, imagine the beam getting bigger or smaller, depending upon how open you want your third eye to be. The more that you control how wide it is the more open it is to receive messages. Remember that, at first, you only want it to be open a little until you get used to the energy and visions that will come through.

As you practice and become use to this, you can open it larger, or you can then close it when you do not want to see or communicate with the angels. When you are done practicing, remember to thank your angels, close your third eye to where you want it, clean your energy, and cut your cords.

Clairaudience is the ability to hear angels. Many times, you may experience this as a ringing noise that may result in words, certain noises, songs, or sayings associated with angels or the messages that one can receive. These messages are usually you or we and are very encouraging and empowering. The voice is clear, blunt and to the point and there is no fear or anger in the message. The message is usually about self-improvement or serving others. There is no harmful message of hurting yourself or others.

One way to increase your ability to hear the angels is to meditate. If you wake up in the morning and sit quietly in meditation and ask the angels to speak to you then, they will. If you have ringing in your ears, simply ask them to turn it down because they are talking at too high of a frequency. Many times, people like to use either clear or pink quartz when they meditate to help them connect. Angels love music and flowers, so having them around you when you meditate allows a peaceful space where you can listen to their message in a stress-free environment. Remember, the more you relax, the easier it is to heal.

Claircognizance is the ability to know something in your guts or mind without knowing how you know it. It is also when someone has an "aha" moment. For example, have you just ever known someone was good or bad when you met them? This means that you could read their energy.

What about knowing when your kids need you? This means that your energy relates to another being. This is truly trusting your instincts.

Other people may just know something happened somewhere and they do not know where they got the information or have such a strong premonition or déjà vu.

To increase this gift, you may learn how to shield yourself with either pink or white light to keep the thoughts from overwhelming you and allowing you to choose when you have premonitions.

You could also wear a rose quartz necklace to help bring in the energy and control your emotions. This gift is the hardest emotionally because you must learn how to separate your thoughts from others. This can be done when meditating and becoming familiar with your voice and the voice of your angels. This is also a way to become familiar with voices that are not as positive or from the light so that you may avoid them.

Clairsentience is when you overcome strong emotions that are not connected to your emotions. You may be extremely happy or sad and have no idea why, or you may feel pain in certain parts of the body, and you have nothing physically wrong with you. Many times, this is a more painful gift because sometimes you may connect with spirits and feel how they died. But, when working with your angels, it will help you feel if you are connected to you or to a passed loved one or a negative entity.

To hone this gift, meditating, as stated above, is a perfect way to separate your emotions. Just set your intention to focus on emotions rather than thoughts. Another way is to ask your angel to not let you "feel" bad stuff but let you know what it is. Remember you have one strong "clair", but others work and, as you develop them, they will become stronger.

Remember, if you start feeling emotions that you do not understand, do not react to them as first. Instead, you should stop, take a breath, and concentrate on the source of the emotion. If it feels familiar, then process it. If it does not, shield yourself and brush it off. Eventually, you will learn how to separate these emotions faster as you practice.

Clairgustance is the least known and one that many people take for granted. It is the gift of smell. This is when you smell perfume, smoke, flowers, air temperature change, food etc. and it is not physically there. Or when you smell a familiar smell, and it reminds you of a certain time, place, or person. These smells may also be associated with the angels or the one with whom you are trying to connect.

Meditation.

Please sit comfortably and relax your body.

› Begin by taking three deep breaths - inhale, exhale, inhale, exhale, inhale, and exhale.

› As we begin to relax, we are going to invite the Archangel Michael into the room for our protection and to ensure that we only encounter higher energies during this exercise.

› As Michael comes into the room, you begin to sense peace and protection.

› As you continue to breathe, you envision yourself in this room all by yourself.

› You sense your energy, and you know that there is something that wants to speak to you. As you begin to step forward, you know that there is something that wants to communicate with you using one of your clairs. As you continue to look around, you are relaxed and are ready to meet the angels in this room.

› You may feel a cool breeze around you or the gentle protection of wings around you. As you feel more comfortable, you reach out to the angels and, as my voice begins to disappear, you begin to sense the angels. I will give you a few minutes to enjoy this experience.........

> Now, as you finish your conversation with the angels, thank them for taking time to speak with you, turn and walk back to your chair and sit. Relax and take a deep breath- inhale and exhale, inhale and exhale and then slowly open your eyes.

What did you see? Feel?

You can meditate and connect with your angels while you are in the shower or bath, while lying in bed, anywhere you can become comfortable and not be interrupted for a moment.

Assignment:

Which clair are you? Most people can connect with two or three but usually one resonates with them more than the others. Choose your clair and research ways that you can strengthen your gift and write these in your Angel Journal. What exercises worked? Which ones did not?

Communicating with the Archangels.

There are many ways besides meditation to communicate with your angels. Though meditation is good not everyone can sit still and focus for that amount of time. So, here I am offering a few other alternatives:

Writing to your angels. Take a piece of paper and write to your angels. You can give thanks, write down anger, fears, or wishes or simply talk to them. This really helps clear the soul of pent-up emotions. This is a safe way to communicate with them while having someone to confide in. After you have written to them, take the paper and burn it. As you burn it and the smoke goes up, envision the words going up into the heavens to allow the angels to take over your pain or to spread your thanks.

Say angel affirmations. You may ask how this is communicating with angels. When you are happy and love yourself then it is easier to see the love and happiness around you. Fear, hate, and doubt keep you from communicating with them. So, each day or when you feel yourself getting upset or fearful, take a few minutes to say or write down positive affirmations for yourself. These can be anything from "I am loved and guided by the angels" or "I am a great soul that is connected to the heavens", etc.

Creating an angel altar. Many people think of altars as worship, but they can simply be a sacred space in your home or office that you create to show respect or to give thanks to the angels. This can be in a room that you deem as a spiritual room where you may meditate or practice your angelic Reiki or communication. You can add and change different objects depending upon what your need for the day is- to cleanse, ground, give thanks, heal, etc. When creating an altar, you may put anything on it that you feel represents the angels that you want to communicate with, what you want to focus or meditate on or bring love to. Items may include feathers, candles, soft music, incense, pictures of loved ones, money, etc. Just allow it to represent what you want. Remember to keep it clean and uncluttered.

Meditate and keep a journal. Many times, people who meditate have a wonderful experience while meditating and shortly after. However, they forget what they have experienced within just a few minutes. When meditating, simply keep a journal near you and, when you stop meditating, write down or draw everything you experienced. This will not only help you preserve the experience, but it allows you to go back and look at what you learned. You may be surprised at either the change within yourself over time OR signs and messages you received that you only realized later.

Channeling messages by connecting with your guardian angel. It is important to develop a strong relationship with your guardian angel so that you may be more aware when they are trying to communicate or send you a message. Here is what you do: take a pen and paper and sit comfortably. Think of a question and then center and calm yourself. As your mind calms, you open your heart and ask for your guardian angel to come to you and allow them to speak to you. Write down what you see and hear or even possibly draw what you see. Do not censor it or worry about it being perfect and note that there is always a bright light around you and what you experience. Once you are done, thank your guardian angel.

What are Auras?

Next, we are going to look at what auras are and what each of the layers mean. When working with the angels, you will use auras to help you read the client and know how to help Reiki them physically, emotionally, or spiritually.

Auras have seven layers and each one has its own function. There are layers that do not move and there are ones that move constantly. Those that do not move are the first, third, fifth and seventh layers. The second, fourth, and sixth move and change.

› The first layer is known as the etheric layer and is next to the body. It is usually a pale gray or blue and holds memories of the physical body.

› The second layer is known as the emotional layer, and it relates to your emotions at the time and the colors are constantly changing.

› The third layer is known as your mental layer. It is fixed at yellow and holds our thought processes.

› The fourth layer is known as the astral layer, and it relates to our heart energy and changes into pastel colors. It connects our lower physical bodies with our spiritual body.

› The fifth layer is knowns at the etheric template and is bright blue. It stays the same and relates to spiritual development

› The sixth layer is known as celestial layer and is where your spiritual connection begins. It can be several feet from your physical body.

› The seventh layer is known at the spiritual layer and is connected to the crown chakra.

How to Sense Auras.

Many times, while working with the angels in helping your client you will want to sense their aura. A client's aura can tell you a lot about where they are spiritually, mentally, physically, and emotionally. By sensing their auras on each layer and then consulting the chart to see the colors meaning, it can really help you understand what is going on with them. We may be able to cover up our true feelings or trick our loved ones in to believing that we are ok, but our aura never lies.

Here is an exercise to sense your aura:

> Have the client stand or lie for this class on a massage bed or couch.

> Stand near your client and make sure that you have put your archangels' symbols into your palm chakra.

> Take a deep breath, relax, and focus on the client's aura field.

> Hold your hands out across the client above them about 18-20 inches and slowly lower them to their body. Focus your eyes and concentrate on your palm chakras.

> Continue focusing and try to sense the edge of the aura. Many times, you will feel a small resistance or even squishiness or change in temperature or energy. Begin moving up and down their body to see how it is shaped.

> Move your hands all over your client's body and make notes on what you see and feel.

> Relax and then try to go to the next layer and so on and so on.

› Note what you see and share with your client at the end of the session. Make suggestions as to what may be some possibilities.

› If you need to cut cords, then please call in Archangel Michael to assist with this.

How to Cleanse Auras?

When working with the aura, you may note either nasty residual energy or cords or even an imbalance in the aura from too much of one layer. These can be fixed in several ways:

› Dry bathe the client with your hands

› Use clear crystal quartz to go around the aura to take away any negative energy and use it to cut cords or attachments that need to be let go

› Use a drum, crystal bowl or any musical instrument's vibration to balance

› Use a pendulum to find the imbalance and then use it to balance the area

› Remember, whenever possible, to start at the head and end at the feet, brushing off negative energy from the body in that direction

Assignment:

Write in your Angel Journal about this experience. Continue practicing.

Color Therapy

We are now going to discuss how to use Reiki with angel colors in this section. Color therapy has been used since the beginning of time and much of it has been experienced subconsciously. The color and vibration help "put the areas" back in a positive vibration. This color therapy can also be applied to the chakra sections that we will be discussing later in this class.

Here we go:

> Red focuses on spiritual devotion through selflessness and is connected to the root chakra. It helps ground you. Uriel is the angel that works with this stone. It helps heal the sex organs, legs, feet, knees, and hips. Using red also helps detoxify the body. Do not use for high blood pressure, hyperactivity, fever, or agitation. Emotionally it helps release energies and helps boost you mentally and emotionally and releases self-obsessive patterns. Spiritually it helps you overcome the material world.

> Orange focuses on creativity, or for getting rid of fear and it helps with the sacral chakra. The archangel Gabriel helps heal with this color as it helps heal physically the lower back, intestines, abdomens, kidneys, and digestion. It is also known to help with fertility. Emotionally it assists in grief, bereavement, and helps increase creativity, optimism, and a positive life view. Spiritually it is uplifting.

> Yellow focuses on wisdom and focuses on the solar plexus. Jophiel is the angel that works with this color. Physically it helps with liver, gallbladder, spleen, stomach, and the digestive system. It breaks down cellulite, removes toxins and helps to heal arthritis, joint stiffness, and immobility. Emotionally it assists with mental agility and learning enhancement, wisdom, and intellect as well as joy and

happiness. It helps prevent shyness, gives courage, and prevents mental confusion. Spiritually it helps illuminate the connection to the higher self, guides, and angels.

› Green focuses on wellness and harmony and on the heart chakra. Raphael is the wellness angel with this color. He uses green to balance, calm, and relax. It helps with tension headaches, migraines, and emotional states of being restricted. It also helps with divine visions and intuition.

› Blue focuses on communication and is assisted by Michael. It helps heal the throat chakra, thus helping with communication and creativity. It helps heal the throat, thyroid, upper lungs, jaw, weight, and the skull. Emotionally it helps you speak your truth and brings peace to you. Spiritually it helps one seek a higher truth and carries the power of faith and protection.

› Indigo focuses on intuition and insight and the third eye chakra. Physically indigo helps with pituitary gland, skeleton, lower brain, eyes, and sinuses. It lowers high blood pressure, back problems, and sciatica problems. Emotionally it sedates the conscious mind and creates an internal communication. It helps you become self-aware and is used to treat obsession. Spiritually it clears negative thoughts and aids in the clairs and psychic development.

› Violet is assisted with growing by Zadkiel. It focuses on self-transformation and spiritual growth and is associated with the crown chakra. It heals the cranial skull and helps with bruises and black eyes. It helps with mentally releasing emotional turbulence. It frees the imagination and helps with meditation and connection to your higher spirit. It cleanses anything it touches.

› White is associated with Metatron and is simply enlightenment. It restores vibrancy and is used for a cure all for anything. You can use white to heal anything. It wipes the slate clean. I use white to purify anything that needs cleansing.

› Pink is associated with Chamuel and is also associated with the heart. It helps heal broken hearts as well as helps with allowing nothing but pure love in rather than block everything out when you are doing readings. It builds confidence and self-esteem.

How to Do a Color Meditation.

› Relax and sit comfortably and close your eyes.

› Begin breathing deeply and inhale and exhale deeply.

› Breathe until the count of three and visualize yourself bringing in the red color and allowing it to hold at your root chakra. Envision Uriel there helping you heal the root chakra. Hold it until it becomes bright.

› Do this with each of the six other chakras and archangels.

› When you are finished you can concentrate on white light and relax and allow it to circle and protect you. Finally, see the white light going from your crown to the heavens.

› Take a deep breath and slowly open your eyes.

What are Chakras?

Chakras are circular balls of energy that are throughout your body. We usually focus on the main seven that start at your tail bone and end at the top of your head.

In order, from the bottom to the top, they are root (tailbone), sacral (below the belly button), solar plexus (below your rib cage), heart, throat, third eye (the center of your forehead), and crown (the top of your head).

How to Sense the Chakras.

When working with a client who wants you to work with their chakras, use this way to sense them. It is quick and easy.

The Archangels that you want to work with are Michael for protection and Raphael for Reiki.

- Have the client lie on the massage table or couch.

- Take a deep breath and charge your palm chakras with the symbols of the above angels.

- Gain connection with your client and place your hands about 8 inches above the root chakra.

- Try to sense the chakra by closing your eyes and feeling the energy coming from the chakra. Does the chakra feel dense and heavy or light and open? If you are a clairvoyant, do the colors look dark and dingy or bright and colorful?

- You can also use a pendulum by holding it above the chakras and asking it if the chakras are open or closed.

- After you do the root chakra, then you continue up the body until you reach the crown chakra.

- Take note of any work that needs to be done on clearing or balancing the chakras.

How to Balance Chakras.

Once you have sensed the chakras and checked to see if they are open or closed, you will begin balancing or cleansing your chakras.

There are many ways of doing this - with your hands/Reiki, with a pendulum, with crystals, etc.

> Using your hands is great, especially if you do not have any tools with you.

> Simply ask Archangel Raphael to come and assist you and then put your symbols in your hand.

> Hold them together and feel the energy flow.

> Once you feel the energy, hold your hands about 6-8 inches from the root chakra and allow the energy to flow.

> If you feel attachments or negative energy, continue to hold or, if you can, pull them from the body and cut.

> If you pull them, seal the area back with your energy.

> You will know when to move to the next chakra.

> Move upwards until you reach the crown chakra.

Assignment:

Write in your Angel Journal about this experience. Continue practicing.

How to Balance Chakras with a Pendulum.

> Simply ask Archangel Raphael to come and assist you.

› Hold your pendulum about 6-8 inches from the root chakra and allow the energy to flow.

› The pendulum will usually move clockwise.

› As it slows down, move to the next chakra.

› Move upwards until you reach the crown chakra.

› Crystals can be used too. I usually use Clear Crystal Quartz because it can mimic the properties of other stones that may be needed for this.

› There are multiple other ways to help balance and clear chakras but, simply put, the focus of clearing chakras is to balance energy and clear negativity, so the tools are more for your preference.

How to Lead Past Life Journeys.

When doing a past life journey we connect with our guardian angel, and Archangels Michael, Gabriel, and our higher self, as well as Metatron who helps us consult our Book of Life.

When you take these journeys, you are usually guided to the past lives that mean the most to you and will help you with your issue in this lifetime. Remember, you can change the future, so this helps when you want to go back and look at your past life.

How to do this:

> Make yourself comfortable and relax.

> Take deep relaxing breaths that calm you with each one.

> As you begin to relax, ask for your guardian angel or whatever angel you chose from the list above.

> Envision you and your guardian angel going through a doorway.

> As you pass through the doorway, envision meeting Metatron. He will be your guide through this journey.

> Once you see him, thank him for taking the time to go with you and allowing you to see the life that you need to help you in this journey.

> Envision him walking with you as you step on a cloud that is like a moving sidewalk.

> After a few moments, you stop because it is time to get off.

> As you step off, look at your feet- you notice that you have changed. Are these men's feet or women's feet? Are you wearing shoes or not? What style or year are the shoes?

> Begin looking at your legs and take in the difference with those? What kind of clothes are you wearing? Can you tell your status? Your job?

> Walk around the room where you are and ask yourself about the type of dwelling you are in? Can you tell the era? The country?

> Take time to walk and interact with others. Do you recognize anyone? Many times, people's eyes stay the same, but they may be a male or female. How is this person reacting to you?

> Now, take time to really visit this past life with no judgment. About 15 minutes.

> Once you have a clear idea of this past life, or want to return, simply turn to Metatron, and thank him for his guidance and ask your guardian angel to come home.

> As you step through the door with your guardian angel, remember to not be judgmental about anything that you saw. This is to help you see how far you have come and what you still must work on.

> Now, slowly thank your guardian angel and walk towards the light.

> Breathe slowly and, when ready, open your eyes.

> Now, take time to write in your Angel Journal so you can reflect later.

> This can be used as a meditation to take your clients through a regression. This is the client centered approach.

How to Do Past Life Readings.

A Past Life Reading is different than a past life journey in that it is YOU, the reader, who is focused on seeing the past life, NOT the client. This is where the client is dependent upon what you see and how you interpret the life.

This is good for those that are just curious and would like to be able to confirm what they saw. This one is easy to do:

> Simply put your symbols in your hand and ask Archangels Metatron and Michael to surround you and the client.

> As you take the client's hand, ask them to take a deep breath and to relax.

> Look them in the eye and you relax.

> Let your eyes relax and you will notice that their face will go fuzzy.

> The fuzzier it gets the more you should relax because, in a few moments, you will notice their face morphing.

> Speak what you see- do not be afraid. Remember, no one should judge what you see.

> Talk to the client about what they see and ask if they have any questions. Try to connect as much as you can.

> Once you feel like you have done all that you can, breathe deeply and thank the angels for going with you.

> After the client leaves, remember to cut cords with them.

> This can be done with a mirror as well.

Assignment:
Write in your Angel Journal about this experience. Continue practicing.

How to Connect to Angels Using your Angel Cards.

When picking out angel cards, remember to pick a deck that resonates with you. They may feel good in your hands or tingle, or they may just feel so perfect for you.

Once you get your cards, take them out of the box and clean them from all the energy that they have met. This can be done by touching each card or holding them to your heart and asking Michael to cleanse and protect them. You can also tap them three times, use your angel or Reiki symbols on them, and lay a cloth over them. There are lots of ways of doing this, but remember, it all comes down to intent.

To help get your cards attuned to you many people always suggest either sleeping with them under your pillow or keeping them on you. This just helps your energy be absorbed and helps you connect to them as well.

Also remember that, when it comes to your cards, people ask if you should let the client touch, or cut or choose a card- that is up to you. Some readers NEVER let people touch their cards, while others could care less.

Remember, either way, that once you finish the readings you should clear your cards and cut the cords that have developed with your client.

You may find that, once you get a deck of cards, you may want more decks, or you may stick to the trusty one- again, that is up to the reader. Many find that they love the beauty of the decks and just collect them.

How to Do a One Card Angel Reading.

Getting to know your cards is very important. One exercise that I encourage students to do is to pick an angel card each morning and to take a few moments and feel the card in your hand. Can you feel any positive energy? Can you sense what the card is? Take a few moments and concentrate on it. I then ask students to take a few moments and look at the card and hear or see what the message is. Take a few moments to write some notes in your Angel Journal.

Throughout the day, take note of any signs that show what the card was saying.

At the end of the day, look at the card and see what signs or how this card related to your day and write it in your journal.

Do this daily to help you connect with your cards! You can do this for your friends as well!

How to Do Past, Present, and Future Spreads with Angel Cards.

Another basic spread of reading your angel cards is the past, present, and future spread.

› Pick your deck.

› Clear your cards by one of the techniques taught earlier.

› Ask a question to yourself or have your client ask one.

› Shuffle the cards and then choose one card.

› Put it to the left.

› Then choose another card.

› Place it to the right of that card.

› Then choose another card.

› Place that to the right of that card.

› Flip over the card to the farthest left over - this is your past card.

› What does it say? Do you hear anything? Feel anything? This is what is influencing your question.

› Next flip the next card and this is the card or what is influencing your question currently.

› Now flip the last card. This is where your question stands in the future based upon your energy.

› These can also be switched to beginning of the week, middle of the week, and end of the week or now, next month, etc. It is all based on intent.

How to Prepare for an Angelic Reading Session.

It is important to prepare yourself and your client for an angelic Reiki session. Here are some important steps:

› Both of you should wear loose clothing to allow the energy to flow.

› Both of you should drink plenty of water to stay hydrated and to help with the detox process.

› Avoid heavy meals before and after the session.

› Wash your hands with cool flowing water to help cleanse them physically and energetically.

› Relax and you both should remove glasses, jewelry, and objects from your pockets.

› Make the client comfortable by having them lay down on a massage table or couch with soft pillows.

› Make sure the client does not cross their legs or arms but is comfortable.

› Cover the client with a white sheet or blanket.

› Call in the angels and connect with them.

› Connect with the energy flow.

› Do the card or past life reading or regression or color therapy.

› Discuss with the client your findings and messages and help them process this for their life.

› Allow them to sit for a few minutes and offer them some water to keep them from being dehydrated.

Assignment:

Write in your Angel Journal about this experience. Continue practicing.

Setting up a Session.

When beginning as a healer, it is important to follow these steps to ensure that you and your client are protected during the session and that you cleanse yourself when the session is over. As time goes on, you will note what works for you and eventually make this your own. For the first few months, I suggest that you stick to this outline.

Self-treatment. The first thing that you should do is make sure that you are physically and spiritually healthy. Just like with Reiki, if you need wellness then the energy will help you first and then your client. Eliminating a few things from your life, such as alcohol, cigarettes, caffeine, and certain foods, is a good habit for any practitioner in preparing for sessions. Another suggestion is to exercise regularly, meditate, and have a connection to a spiritual outlet that will allow you to let go of negativity and embrace a peaceful energy force. Before each session, you should take a few minutes to perform a mini-Reiki session on yourself and then center yourself. You should also take a moment to meditate and ask the angels to help guide you in this session.

Prepare your room by clearing it. I use my Reiki symbols as well as Archangel Michael's symbol to help strengthen and protect the area. I then set the intention of the session, this can be specific for what the client has told me before hand or generic for a healthy session for your client to receive what he or she needs to heal. Also, say a small prayer for protection and for guidance. You may also use sage or incense as well.

Charge your room. Charge your room with the symbols that you will be attuned to. If you have Reiki or other energy modalities, you can incorporate these symbols as well. While doing this, invite Archangels Michael, Raphael, and any other angels that you work with to come into the room and to lead you.

Choose meditation music beforehand. You can pick and choose what the client needs to hear. Many times, the client is stressed, and the guided meditations help them relax. You can ask them which they prefer but have both handy before the client arrives.

Light candles to help invite the angels. When working on clients, white candles are the ones that invite angels but remember to choose colors that coordinate with your angels, as well as your chakras and how they help heal your body.

Lay out your crystals that you may use on the client or in the room. You can create a crystal energy grid or use them on the client during your session. Clear crystal quartz is my favorite and it has been called the crystals of the angels. It is also good because clear crystal quartz can also take on the property of other crystals that may be used for Reiki traditionally.

Shield yourself with the pink light of Archangel Michael. Imagine Archangel Michael sending pink light down to you through your crown chakra and down through your body and out your feet. Imagine it taking the ick and nastiness with it and coming back up through your feet and out of your crown chakra and then envision it surrounding you like a bubble. Many ask why pink rather than white? White keeps out everything and pink allows only love and positive energy in. This is a perfect shield for readings and Reiki sessions.

Gain rapport with your clients. When the client arrives, build rapport with them by asking them what they need and allowing them to explain to you their issues and what they think has caused the issues. Really listen to them. The worst thing is to let your client say one word and then jump in and act like you know everything about them and you can cure them. They know their body and are the best experts.

Complete Paperwork. Have them fill out an information form on what is wrong or what they want to work on. Also allow them to sign a disclaimer stating that they understand that you are not a doctor, and you promise nothing regarding curing them or taking the place of medical advice. Also remember that in many states, unless you are a medical practitioner with a license or a minister, you cannot "touch" anyone. You do not have to physically touch a client for them to receive the Reiki energy. Remember to keep things legal and safe.

Relax the client. Have the client sit in a chair or lay on the massage table and help them relax. Ask them to close their eyes and to open themselves to receiving Reiki. This may be accomplished by a dim room, music, aromatherapy, guided imagery, or by simply talking to the client. Once they are relaxed, then you may begin the session.

Placement of symbols. Begin by placing the symbols in your hand and above the client and set your intention for the session. Remember your clairs and activate them. You can either see, hear, feel, or just know where you need to go. Incorporate these with the following techniques.

Scan the body. Begin by scanning the body (from head to feet) to see where the Reiki is needed. Your palm chakras are open, and you should be able to feel the change in energy as you come closer to the body as well. Feel for any irregularities in the body; do you feel heat or cold or anything icky or hard? This is where the Reiki needs to take place. Once you find these spots, simply place your hands there and ask Archangel Raphael to help you heal. (If you just feel that a place needs Reiki, then it probably does- trust your angels to guide you). Once you are done with one spot, move to the next spot and so on and so on until you have done the entire body.

Scanning the body. Another way to find where Reiki is needed is to scan by using your eyes. Use your eyes to look and see if there are places where the aura or energy is darker or places that have holes or cords coming out of it. Concentrate there to send Reiki to your client. You can beam the Reiki energy to the client with your eyes or use you breathe to send the energy.

Hand positions. There are standard hand positions that many people use. These are good if you are new and you like to stay structured; but, as you become more comfortable, you can mold this to what you feel comfortable doing. The hand positions begin at the head and go to the client's feet. Begin with the crown, then the eyes, ears, back of the head, throat, shoulders, chest, solar plexus, sacral, lower back, hips, legs, knees, and feet. Some people have clients flip over. I prefer to stoop under the table and send the energy that way. This keeps me from disturbing the client by having them flip over and lose the relaxing moment. No matter what you choose, please remember to end at the feet and to push the yuckiness away from the body. Then end by dry bathing the body.

Attachments. While you are working on the client, notice if there are any negative energies or attachments to the client. Use your "clairs" to know if they are there or simply asking Raphael to guide you. If you find attachments, then ask Archangel Michael to help you cut the cords and Archangel Raphael to heal the area.

Seal the area. When you are finished, seal the area around the body and push the energy to the feet. Then apply Archangel Michael's symbol over the client's solar plexus.

Ending the session. When you feel as if you have either completed the session or the session time has run out, gently touch the client. Let them know to take a few deep breaths and, when they are ready, they can sit up.

Angel cards. Once they sit up, take your angel deck, and clear the deck and ask the client to choose a card. This is their angel message. Discuss the message with the client and see what other messages the angels send to you.

Cleansing yourself. After the client leaves, dry bathe yourself, cut cords to your client, and cleanse your room.

Assignment:

Write in your Angel Journal about your experiences with your first session. What did you like? What do you want to change? Use this as a reflection for your first session.

Treating Animals, Plants, the Planet, and the Universe.

You can use this energy modality to help heal the world around you by asking the angels to help with animals, plants, the planet, and the universe. To do this, you can use many of the same techniques that you used above on your clients.

For example, if you are working with domesticated animals, you can either scan or beam over them to find where they need Reiki and send the energy that way. Remember to never just walk up to a pet and start doing Reiki. Ask for permission from the owner before you proceed and then explain to the owner and to the pet what you are doing. If the animal is wild, ask the animal permission before doing Reiki and then try beaming the energy to them. Always call the humane or wildlife society so that they can do what they are trained to do. Do not approach wild animals! Always use caution when working with unfamiliar animals.

If you are wanting to Reiki plants, you can scan to see what is needed or simply just meditate in nature and send the Reiki from you to the plants around you, into the earth or out into the universe. Just focus on seeing Michael and Raphael with you and allow them to help you with their Reiki energy.

Remember that you also have a voice to talk with and to sing with, and animals, plants and yes, the planet loves music! Music soothes and heals everyone and everything, so use your voice to heal everything around you.

Many times, we forget that animals, plants, earth, and the universe are all living beings, and we love talking to each other, so remember to talk to them as well. This positive energy helps everything around us.

A good suggestion to help nature or large groups is to hold Reiki circles or meet-ups and invite friends and the community to come together and connect with the Archangels to send Reiki to what the circle decides to focus on.

Assignment:

Attend or organize a Reiki circle that focuses on the earth, or pets, or anything that you wish. Write in your Angel Journal about your experiences and ideas.

Distant Reiki

Students ask me all the time "I have a sick friend in another state, how can I help them?" or "I know someone who needs help, but we can't connect, what can I do?" Well, this is simple, just do distant reiki. The archangels can be asked to go anywhere, even via time and space. So, here are a few things that you can do to help send Reiki to those you love. Please remember, when possible, to ask permission to send them Reiki. We cannot force this on people. However, in emergency situations, this may not be possible. There are situations where the person or client cannot respond. In this case use your common sense.

Using objects. When someone requests Reiki and they are not there in person, you can use an object to represent them. Objects that you can use may include photos, teddy bears, dolls, and a paper with the person's name on it, or anything that will help you visualize the person. Simply take the object in one hand; and, with the other hand, do the symbol that you want to use above the object and ask for the archangel that is associated with that symbol to go help that person. Then say a prayer regarding the intention to the specific situation and thank them for their assistance.

Reiki through space and time. Reiki in the present is not the only distant Reiki that you can do. Many times, issues from the client's past or even past life are what is causing the issue in the present. So, with the help of your client, you may choose to work with them to see what in their past triggered this issue or what needs to be forgiven or worked through. Once you can identify that, then you can send Reiki to the past to where it can help them there and, as a result, help them in the present.

Another issue that others have is fear of the future. This may be something specific, such as surgery, a health-related situation or something more emotional, such as a situation they don't look forward to dealing with or even an interview for a job that they really want. In this situation, have your client look at and examine why there is so much anxiety. Then focus on what the client can do to help alleviate this issue.

To help with either situation, simply have them sit down and either draw or write about the past or future situations that are causing them health, mental or spiritual issues. Take this paper and help them meditate on this. As they do this, draw the Archangel symbols that you choose to use and ask them to help by providing Reiki to this situation. Pray/meditate with them and ask Michael to walk with them to help them work through this situation. Then have them continue working on their fear or issue and, if needed, recommend other resources or have them continue working with you to help them through the situation.

Remember that Archangel Raphael is for Reiki and Archangel Michael is for protection, but the Archangels are not limited by our mind or labels. I always ask for both and remember that Reiki may be used for the mind, body, and/or soul.

Remember that Reiki is NOT a substitute for medical, legal, or psychiatric experts. They should always be consulted first.

Beaming Chi Balls. Many times, you will hear the term beaming chi balls. These are focused Reiki that a practitioner can send to a client over space and time. You can arrange with a client a specific place and time for them to be waiting to receive Reiki and you can send it to them by beaming with your eyes on a map or a piece of paper with the address, date and name written on it. All they must do is be open to receive and you just send it at that time with the specified time and place in your directions. It is as simple as that.

This section always amazes students, but you must remember that Archangels and energy are fluid, and they are not bound by time and space.

At the end of any of the above sessions, remember to cut your cord and to dry clean yourself just to ensure that there are no unnecessary attachments.

Assignment:

Journal about your first Distant Reiki Experience. Who or what did you choose to send energy to? What angel did you call upon? How did you feel? Did you get any feedback from anyone?

Cleaning Spaces.

When asked to clean a person's home or space, I ask the archangels to help me with cleaning the space around me, as well as protecting those that are in that home or space. I have used this to prepare my rooms at the mystical fairs, to charge my classrooms at the beginning of the semester to make sure that students are open to learning, as well as when I am going into a new situation and am nervous. In these situations, charge these places like you would your room where you are working on clients. Simply draw the symbols on the wall and do a prayer to ask the angels to come and bring positive energy with them. Other tools that you may use are sage, incense, pendulums, drums, or anything that you use to work with energy. This does help clean the air and bring about a positive experience for the area and those in the area.

Being a paranormal investigator, as well as a metaphysical practitioner and reader, I tend to use my senses more than equipment. For me personally, I am not out to prove or disprove the existence of the paranormal because I know that it exists. My purpose is to help people clean their houses of negative energy and to fill it with the energy of the angels. When I am asked to go to a house and to "see" if there is negative energy or to cleanse the house, I, of course, ask the angels to accompany me for protection and guidance. With their strength in this, I feel that I am ready to help the homeowners.

I ask the angels if there are spirits there that want to cross over, and I then ask Azrael to guide them to the light. But, if there are spirits there that do not want to cross over and they are ok, and the clients are ok having them, then I do not force them. If the clients are afraid, then I will ask them to move to another location or to stop the scaring, etc. Most of the time, if they are a happy spirit and the families are ok, it all works out.

But, if it isn't as simple as this, or it is just residual energy, I cleanse the area as described above and use the Archangels' signs to seal them out and to seal the house with protection, love, and peace.

This can also be done on an object that one feels is haunted or even to get negative energy off someone. You take the object and use the symbols over the object and use the energy to clear the object. You then ask Michael to take the negative energy from the object and infuse it with light.

If the situation appears to be a negative entity or a baddie, I choose not to deal with them and call-in others that have more experience with this to help me or to take over. This is where you let go of your ego and you let each person with their special gifts do their jobs.

Remember to always thank the spirit who cooperated and the humans who asked you and remember that both still have feelings. Confrontation and threats have no place in this situation. Angels see that as ego based and may choose not to assist.

When you leave, please remember to dry bathe and to cut any cords or attachments that you may feel.

Ethics with cleaning spaces or working in other peoples' homes is very important and will be discussed in a couple of sections. The first and most important thing is to never take money for your clearing services. If they offer to donate money for your gas or food that is ok but never charge. This is a situation that most all investigators have agreed upon and it keeps issues from popping up.

Secondly, if you do not see anything, then tell them that. Never fake or lie about what you see or feel. In this case you can refer them to someone else or you could cleanse the area and let the clients know that they should keep a record if they see anything else and then contact you and then you can go from there.

Third, never ever fake noises, events, etc.! There is no excuse to scare people ever!

And finally, be honest with them about what they may be contributing to the situation. There are lots of things that bring in or allow negative energy to flow or attach to you or a place.

So, in these cases, simply remember that you are not the superhero and that the angels are there to help you. You must also use common sense and be careful!

Attunements.

Each student in this class will receive the symbols to Michael, Raphael, Uriel, and Gabriel. Each attunement builds upon itself and only helps the practitioner to become stronger. See the previous symbol chart. Michael and Raphael will be for this level and Uriel and Gabriel will be given to you at the end of level two at the end of this class.

The attunements go into the palm chakras and can be turned on just by the practitioner thinking of the symbol or drawing in on their palms. This simply allows the archangels energy to go through this person and out of their hands to heal the person, etc.

The symbols are not secret, but they are sacred. Please never drink or use mind altering drugs when working with the angels, this usually leaves one susceptible to not feeling the lower or negative energies and not realizing that one may not be working with angels.

Also remember that, even though you are attuned to the angels, you DO NOT control or command them. Always say please and thank you and know that they do not interfere with your free will either.

The attunements and this ceremony also hold the promise that you will never impose your will on others by trying to force heal them, and that you will always be honest and do the best that you can within your power. Remember that you are only human as well and you do not control everyone's destiny.

As the master, I will send you the attunement distantly if you are taking this class online. If you are taking this class in person, I will take each student and attune them individually in a quiet room. Once I pass these symbols from me to you, then you can begin working with the Archangels.

Because of taking on clients, you are opening yourself up for business and legalities which we will talk about next.

How to Run a Successful Business.

You may choose to open a physical business, attend metaphysical fairs, or just work on your friends and family; but, either way, you must have a clear way to run your business.

First, decide where you are going to see clients, such as fairs, office, or home. Each one of these have very specific issues to think about. Here are a few points that will make your business successful no matter where you choose to run it.

First, the issue of money. This is something that many healers have always struggled with when working with clients. Yes, we do this because we want to help people, but we must remember that many times clients want to give us something in return for helping, otherwise they may feel indebted or guilty. So, how do we set a price for services? You can take donations, exchange services or items, such as cakes and pies or maybe your favorite book. Or you can simply get over the issue of money and see your services as valuable to you and charge the average rate in the area in which you are practicing. Either way, money is not evil and should not be viewed as the "be all end all" of everything either. View your services as worthy and others will too. It is as simple as that.

Second, the issue of ethics. Ethics are very important for any business, but it is also very important for a business that hopes to help people improve their mind, body, and soul. Ethically you should never promise to cure anything. We are here to help the angels and the body help itself. Unless you are a medical professional, you should never claim to cure anything or suggest they go off medication. This can result in a lot of legal issues.

Also, ethically speaking, you should not string along clients. In other words, when one issue is over and they are at a spot where they could either stop coming or slow down to every month or so, don't "make up" an issue to get them to become dependent on you. Many of your clients have serious trust or codependency issues and you are there to help them, NOT make it worse. When it is time for them to move on or to take a break, please allow them to do so. They will return to you when they need you again or they may find others that may help them with what they need at that time. Either way, you have both received a gift from each other. This energy is very positive, and others will know by this that they can trust you.

Now, that we have the ethics together, how do you get these clients that you will treat wonderfully? You need to advertise, and you can do this in several ways. Print options are newspapers, fliers, metaphysical magazines, college newspapers, or billboards. Online options are social media outlets such as Facebook and Twitter. Websites and blogs are very important as well. It is very important to update these daily. And finally, the best advertisement is by word of mouth. The more respectful and caring that you are then the more your clients will send you other clients. Remember honesty, kindness, and compassion will get you far.

Unique ways of gaining clients are by doing free energy evenings or an energy circle. Many people are scared or don't understand exactly what Angel Reiki is, if they can come with friends and sit in on a free demonstration or session this may lessen the anxiety issues and possibly open them up for future one on one sessions. You can also offer free sessions at nursing homes, club houses at luxury apartments or the country club, hospitals, libraries, colleges, etc. These are fun places to do the sessions while connecting with a part of the public that may not know what Angel Reiki is or that you even offer it.

And finally, attend metaphysical fairs and hand out information to attendees. Even if you don't feel comfortable or you don't like to do sessions out in a public place, you can still buy a booth and give out business cards, free vouchers or sell gift certificates.

Do not just stop there, there are so many more ways to get the word out about what you do. Contact the media and offer to speak to them on the noon show, do an interview for the newspaper, or write an article for online news sources or metaphysical magazines. Invite the media to an event that you are at and do not be shy. You would be surprised at how many people are open to alternative energy.

While doing all the above, do not forget to sign up to do seminars, workshops, and panels about Angel Reiki. This will really get the word out and bring in clients.

Remember, one of the best ways to bring in clients is by manifesting them. Have the power thoughts that you will be successful and that you will be doing what you love. When people see you doing what you love, then they will come to you.

Good luck and may the angels be with you!

Assignment:

Either journal or create a list or vision board showing what you want to do with your new Reiki attunements. Is there a business that you can envision? What are your goals? Use the Angel Journal to create your dream and talk about which angels you are wanting to work with and how.

Conclusion - How to Receive your Attunements

If you have purchased this book and you are wanting a distant attunement and certificate, the fee is $25. Please email me at anewyouselfcare@gmail.com for this service.

If you are at an in-person class, I will be there to do it for you person to person.

If you are in my online class or working on your own at home, you will receive your attunements via chi ball, which means that you will email me when you feel that you are ready and give me the date and time that you want me to send it. I will then send the attunements to you when you are ready and open to receive it. You will then be attuned.

Here is a list of classes that are available through an online platform on my website:

1. Usui Reiki 1, 2, and 3 Certification
2. Usui Reiki 1, 2, and 3 Certification for Yoga Teachers
3. Nurturing Your Inner Child Shadow Work Workshop
4. Kundalini Reiki Certification Class
5. Animal Reiki Certification Class
6. Spiritual Reiki Certification Class

More classes may be found at www.anewyouselfcare.com

But, for purchasing this book, I am providing you with this free online repository of meditations, journal prompts, and self-care prompts. You may find this class here https://classroom.google.com/c/MTA1Mjk5MzE3MjI2?cjc=24hwbtr

I hope to see you all soon at a virtual class one day!

Namaste!

About the Author

Bertena Varney is an Angel Reiki Master, Usui Reiki Master, Reiki Grand Master, Karuna Ki Reiki, Personal Trainer, Pilates Teacher, Certified Mindfulness Meditation Teacher, Certified Life Coach, Certified Self Care Coach, Certified Health and Wellness Coach, Certified Weight Loss Coach, and is a 500 Hour Yoga Techer. She is the owner of A New You Self Care and Wellness Center, Inner Bliss Spiritual Center, and Midnight Musings with Bertena.

She was an Associate Professor of Sociology in Kentucky. She attended Morehead State University where she received her bachelor's and master's in social science and education, and a master's in sociology and criminology where she focused on cultures, religion, and counseling.

www.ingramcontent.com/pod-product-compliance
Ingram Content Group UK Ltd.
Pitfield, Milton Keynes, MK11 3LW, UK
UKHW040028200726
13854UKWH00001B/423